Challenging spot the difference

starts easy

gets harder!

Over 60 timed puzzles to test your skills!

Illustrated by Giulia Lombardo, Marc Parchow,
Andrea Ebert, & Nicolae Negura

Designed by Ben Potter & Anton Poitier

D1509680

BARRON'S

First edition for the United States and Canada published in
2017 by Barron's Educational Series, Inc.

All inquiries should be addressed to:
Barron's Educational Series, Inc.
250 Wireless Boulevard
Hauppauge, NY 11788
www.barronseduc.com

ISBN: 978-1-4380-0980-3
Date of Manufacture: November 2016
Manufactured by: Shenzhen Caimei Printing Co, Ltd.,
Shenzhen, China
Printed in China
9 8 7 6 5 4 3 2 1

Get spotting!

This book is jam-packed with amazing spot the difference puzzles, which start easy and get harder as you go through the book. Every puzzle has a key at the top of the page with the number of differences to find and a time challenge for you to beat. Look out for this symbol:

Number of differences between the two pictures.  Beat the clock! Time challenge to beat.

The clock is in minutes and seconds. Use a watch with a second hand, or a mobile phone timer to check your time from start to finish. You could write down your time on each page.

TIP! Use a ruler to slide down the picture to isolate one area at a time. This might help to spot some of the differences.

If you like, you can also color the puzzles. Many of them are partially colored and you can complete the blank areas with colored pencils.

The solutions are at the end of the book, in case you get really stuck!

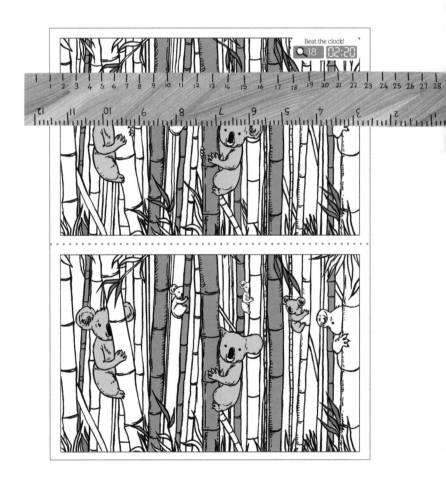

On your mark, get set, go!

Beat the clock!

10 02:15

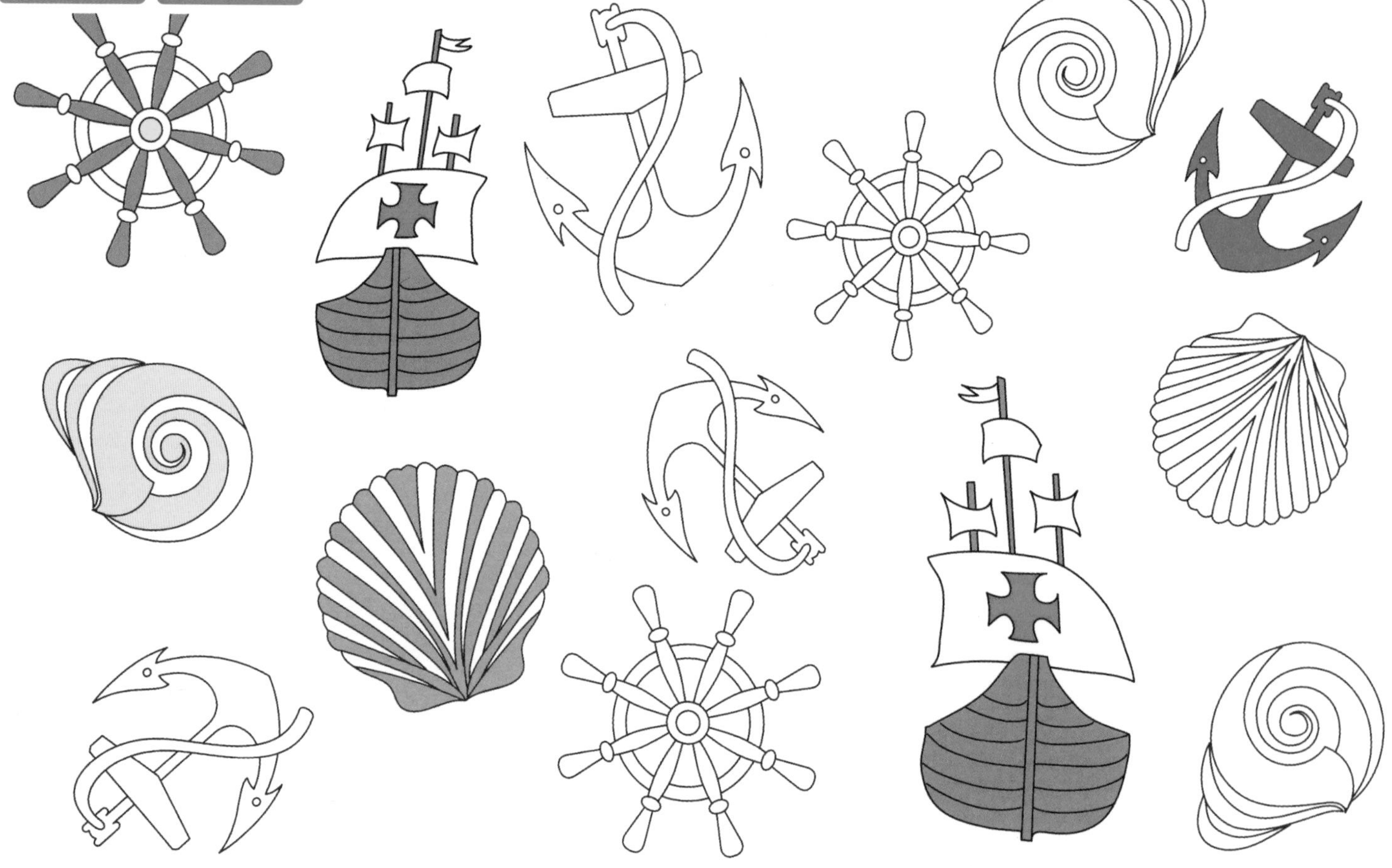

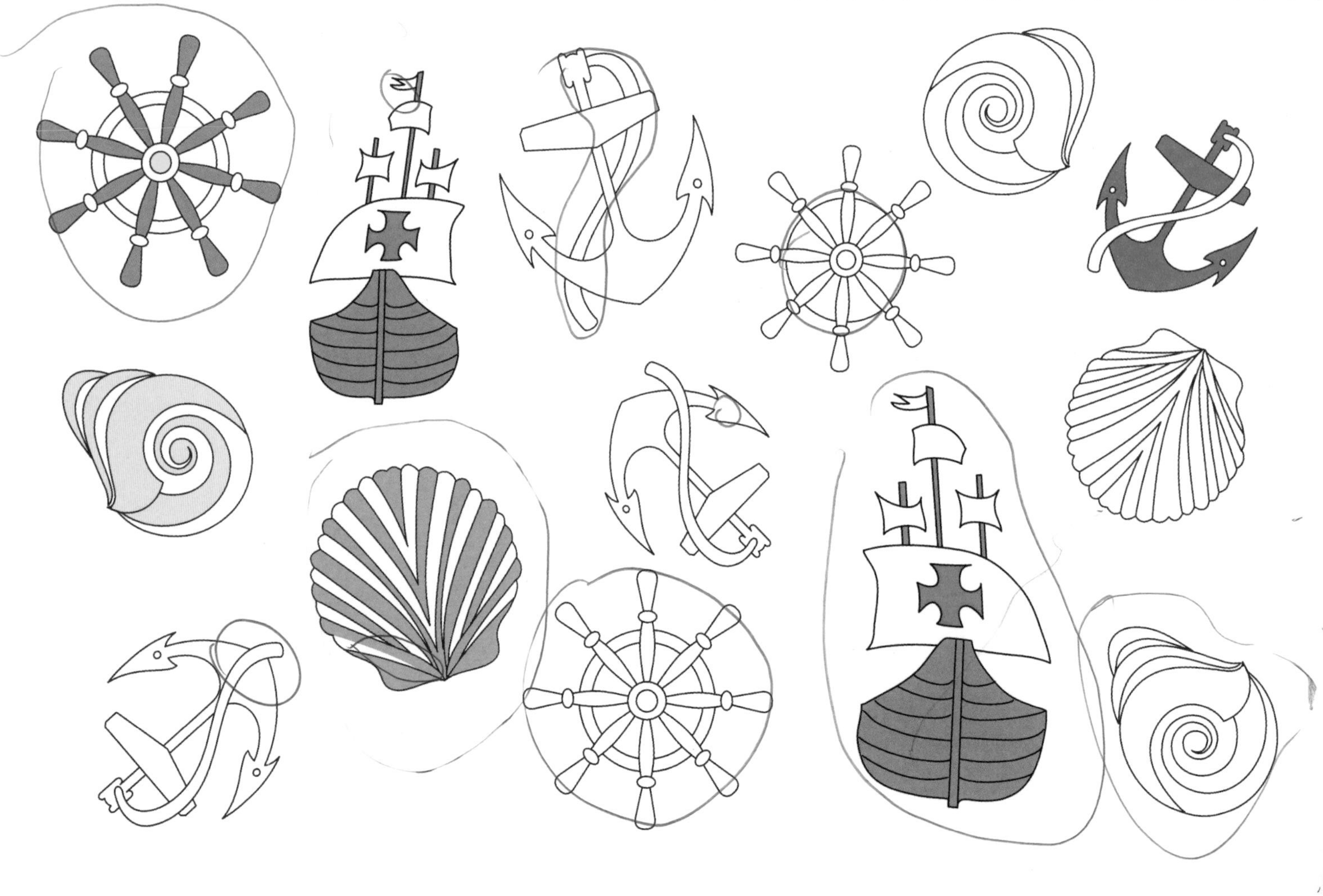

Beat the clock!

42 04:50

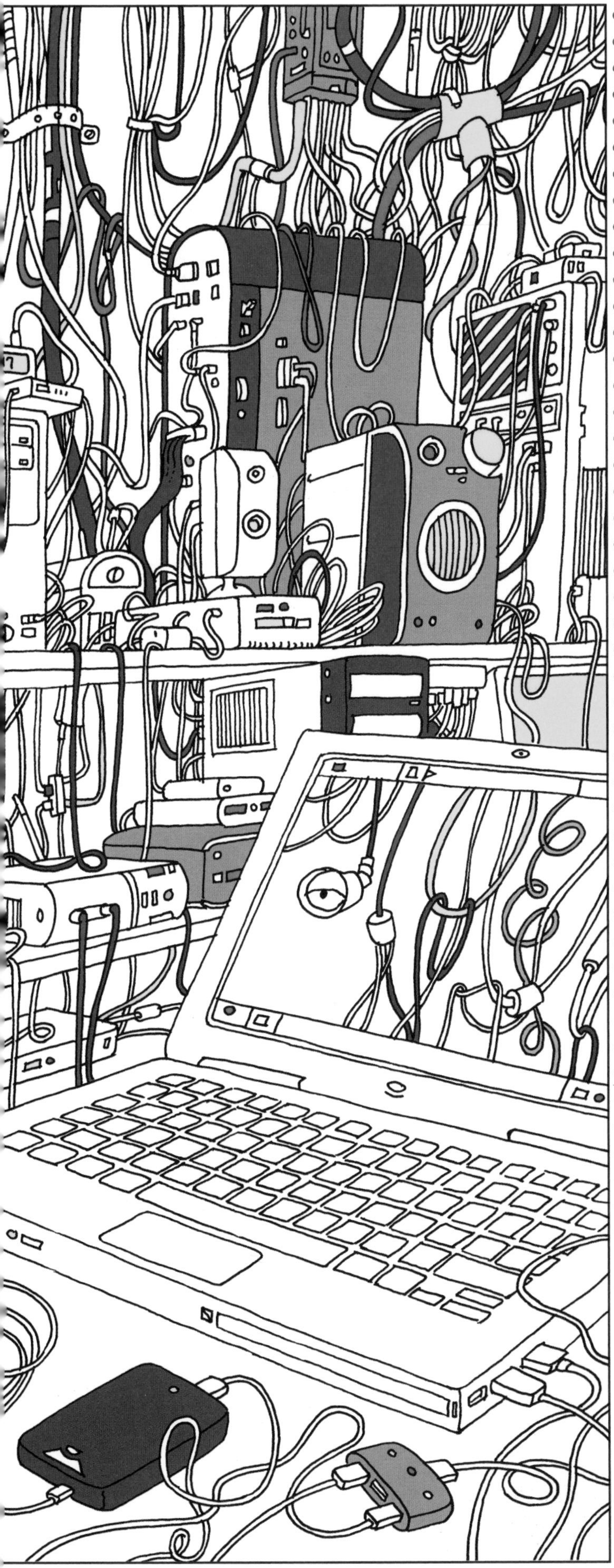

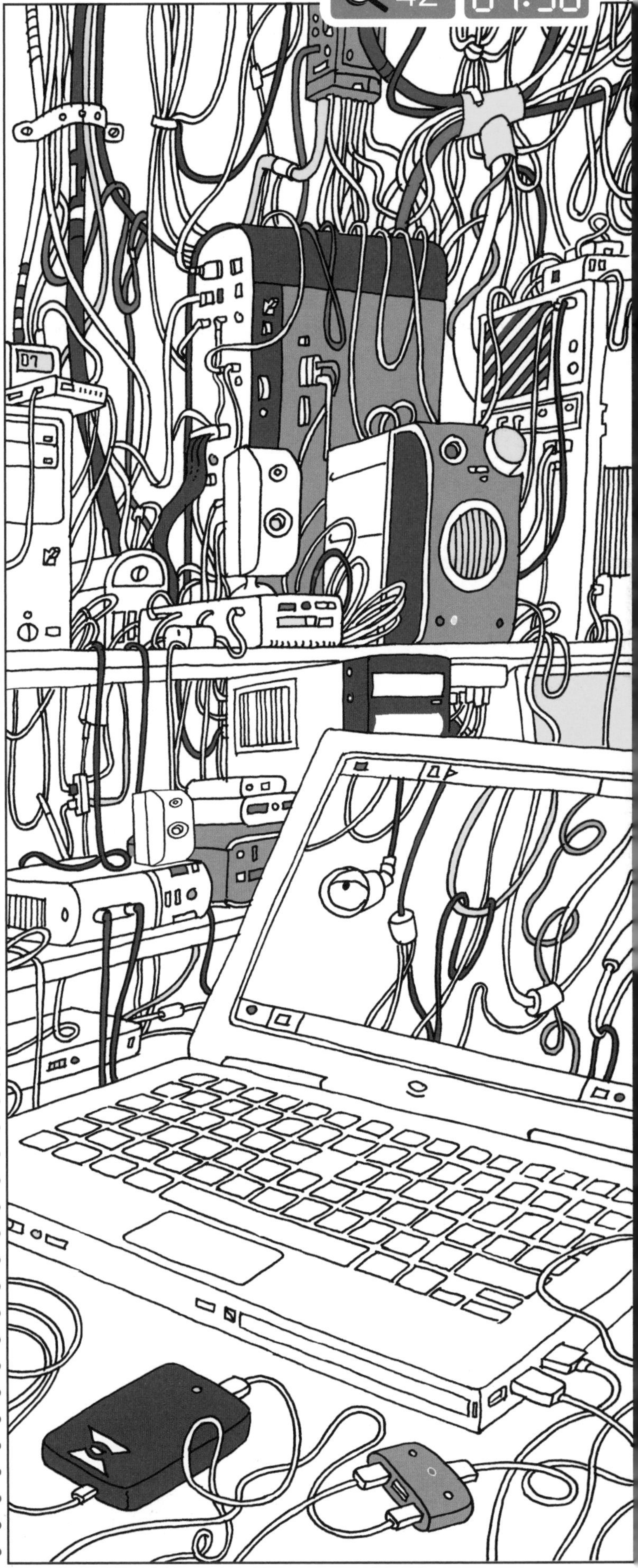

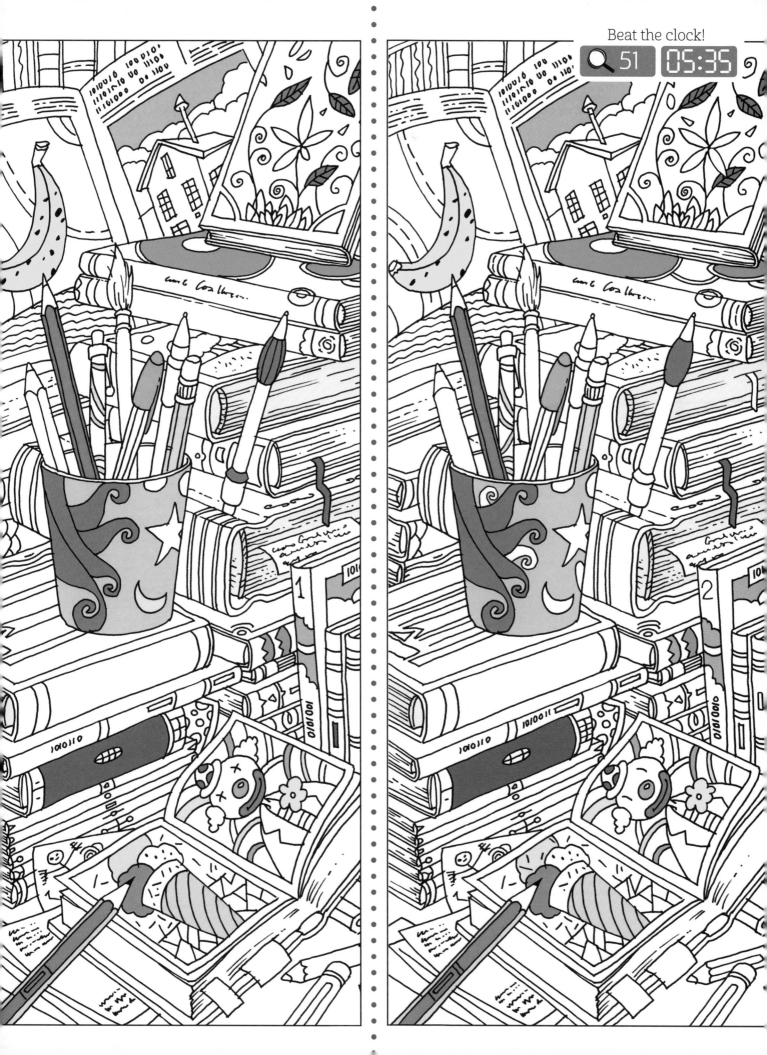

Beat the clock!

69 06:45

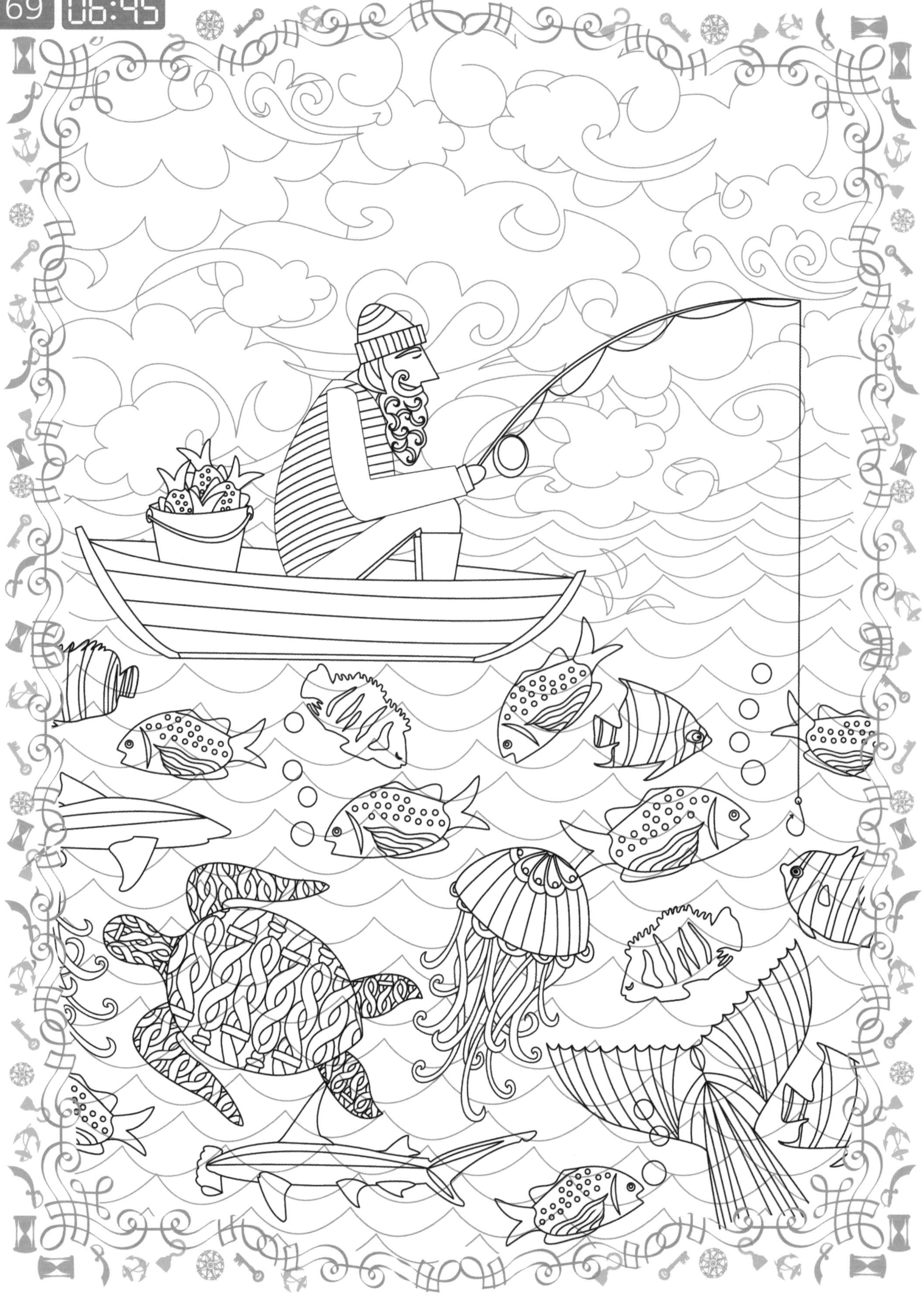

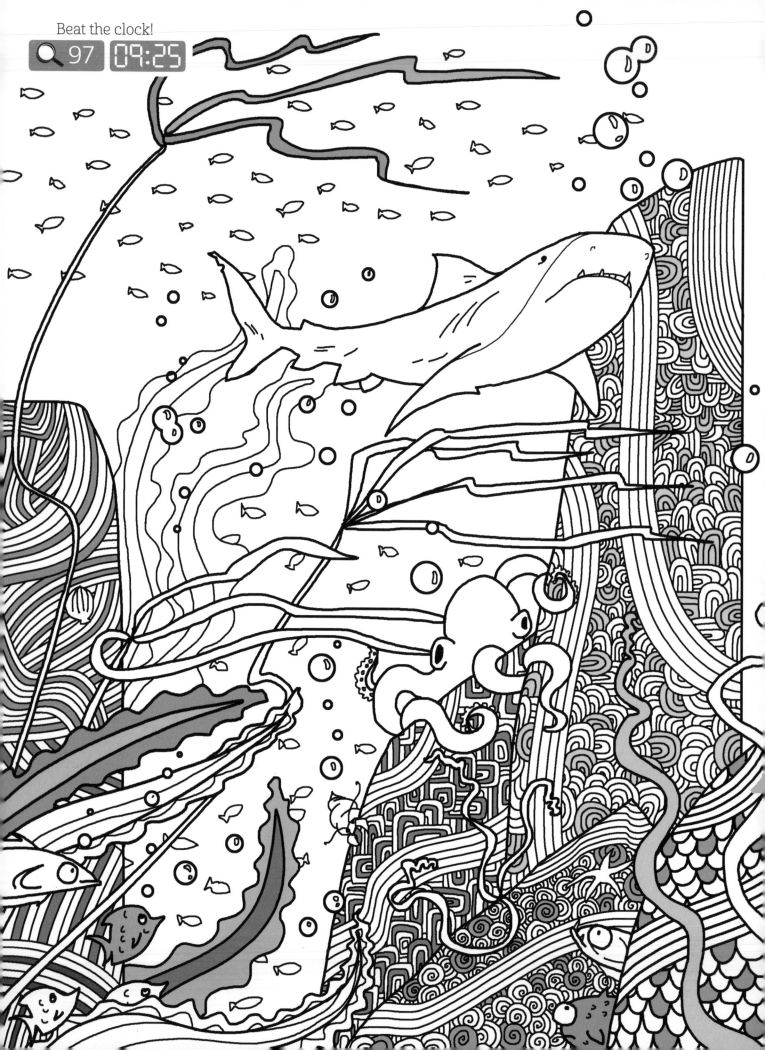

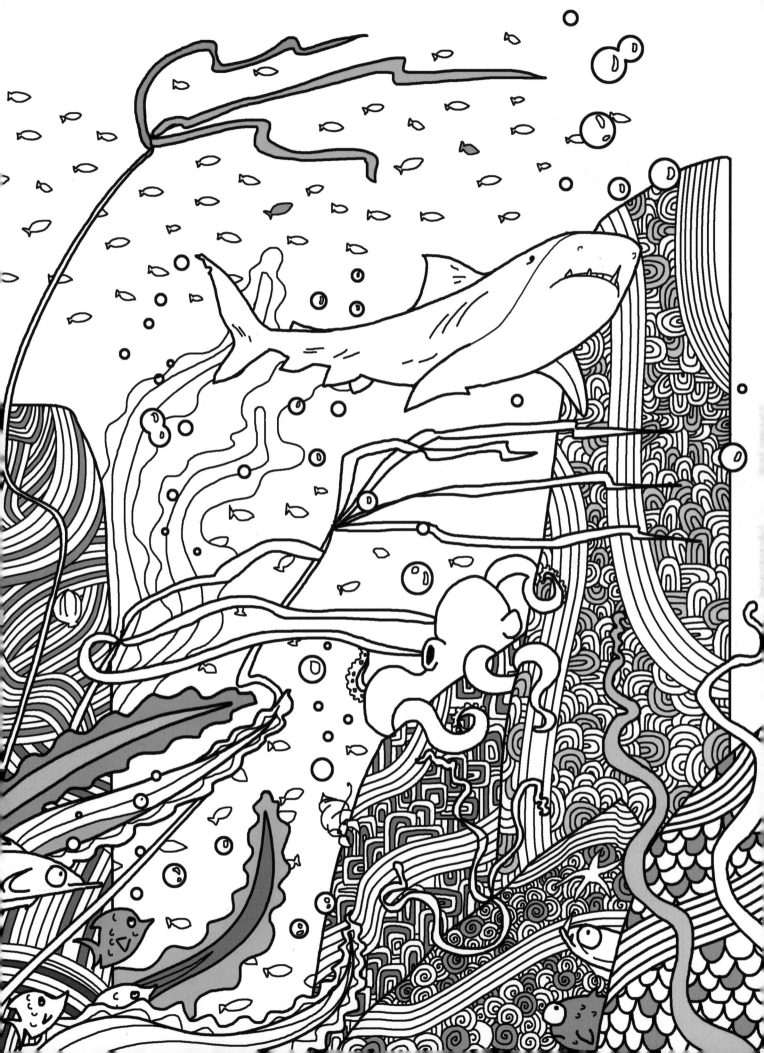

Terminal

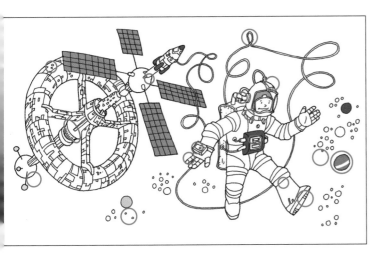

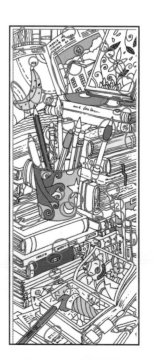

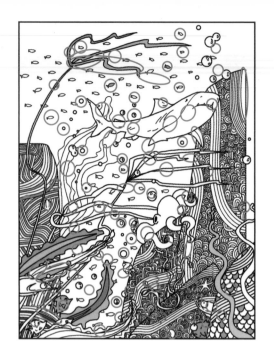